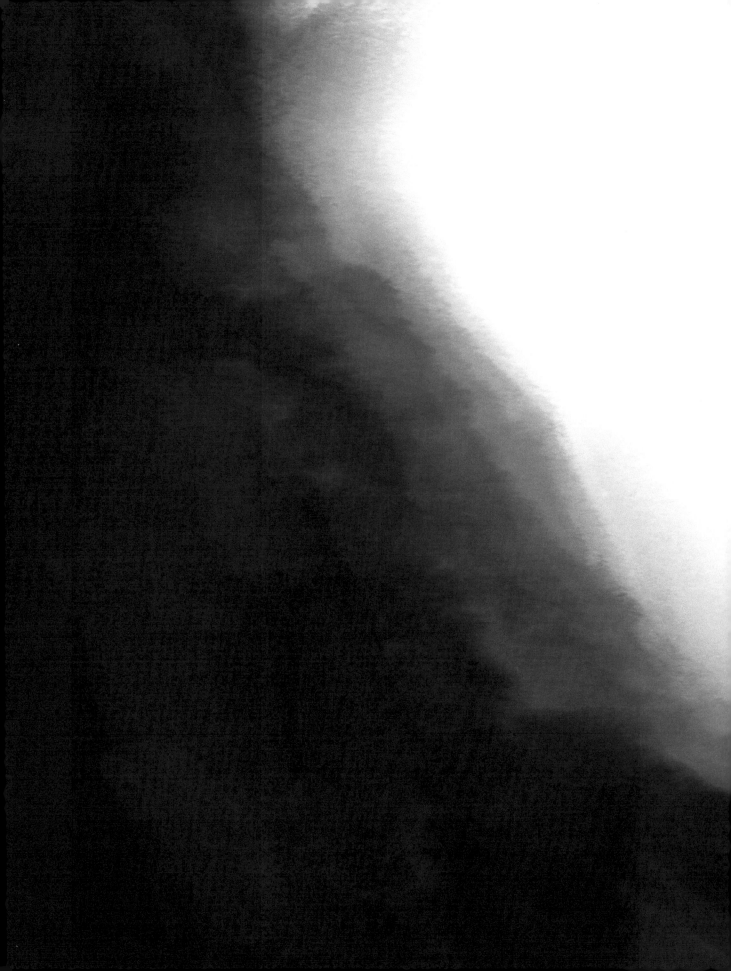

This book is dedicated to

Kimberley

My best friend and favourite person. The one who is busy actually doing all the stuff with the kids instead of just writing about it.

Scriptures quoted are from the Good News Bible © 1994 published by the Bible Societies/HarperCollins Publishers Ltd UK, Good News Bible© American Bible Society 1966, 1971, 1976, 1992. Used with permission.

British Library Cataloguing-in-Publication Date.
A catalogue record for this book is available from the British Library.
ISBN 978-1-5272-8790-7

Printed in Great Britain by DJE Creative.
Illustrations are © Hopefully Made

"Clearly and carefully written and beautifully illustrated, Creation to Crib is an advent resource that can truly be accessed and enjoyed by all ages. Highly recommended!"- **Bob Hartman (The Rhyming Bible and The Lion Storyteller Family Bible)**

"It's rare to find a resource that can engage all ages and abilities together - but this really hits the spot. It looks beautiful, the content is excellent and it's a brilliant way to connect with the Bible and connect with each other. You can adapt for as much or as little time as you have and it even works on short attention spans! I highly recommend it for everyone, especially for families wanting to get started or go deeper in meeting with God together." - **Abby Guinness, Head of Spring Harvest**

"Creation to Crib is a versatile and exciting devotional suitable for use with all ages. Families will enjoy exploring each day's content and suggested activities together, and joining in prayer as they speed through the whole arc of Bible history in the advent season. With stunning illustrations that will draw readers into the story, it is a delightful little book and I'm pleased to commend it." - **Liz Carter, (Catching Contentment and Treasure in Dark Places)**

"David Sims has produced a resource that will help families to pray together with the focus being on the Bible.This resource is helpfully ordered into the 25 days of advent, each subdivided into five sections; Bible Passage, Devotions, Pray, Think, Do. This attractive book covers the 25 day period of advent...to help parents (or grandparents or carers) to walk with their child through the season up until Christmas day. I sense that this approach will help parents and carers to offset the cultural pressure that simply focuses on commercialism and holidaying and will invite the Christian family to capture the true essence of Christmas...that began long ago in the Jewish Bible. It is well designed with clear guidance and useful illustrations." - **Rev Dr Howard Worsley, Assistant Principal @ Trinity College Bristol, and Author (A Child sees God, How not to totally put your children off God.**)

ABOUT THIS BOOK

So many of us struggle to find time and energy to reflect on Scripture, especially through the seasons of Advent and Christmas. We would love to take time with stories from the Bible, but sometimes life is too exhausting and our family situation too difficult. Creation to the Crib is a resource that will help people come together to explore more of God's word through a series of 25 advent reflections tracing the Christmas story all the way from – you've guessed it – the creation of the world through to the crib in Bethlehem.

This book is part of a series I envisioned when I felt God was inviting me to explore a response to Ephesians 4:12, where Paul urges us to 'equip the saints for the work of ministry, for building up the body of Christ.' Some of us are saints within couples. Some of us are saints within a friendship group. Some of us are crawling, some walking, some running – and some bedbound. So how can we make sure that every single saint, each and every person of God, is equipped for ministry?

The Equip project is a devotional series which looks to equip people of all ages and stages of faith. These devotions will speak to those engaging with a boisterous toddler who can't sit still for more than thirty seconds, or with a laid back, cup of tea drinking grandparent. They will enable exploration with thoughtful introverts, whilst connecting with raving energetic extroverts.

The questions will challenge a Christian who knows their Bible better than the Archbishop, as well as someone who goes to church occasionally when they're dragged along. Instead of being restricted to a narrow formula, they are more of a pick and mix to be adapted to the context, the person, and even the time of day.

I pray that, as you engage with this material, you meet with Jesus – the one who holds all of time and history together, and the one for whom we live, breathe, and have our being. Come Holy Spirit!

HOW TO USE THIS BOOK

The best way to use this book is, quite simply, whichever way best helps you get to know more about Jesus. For some, it might look fairly formulaic – beginning with the bible passage and reflection, and choosing one of the Think, Pray, or Do section as a way of putting it into practice. But there are other ways too. Perhaps you might want to begin your day with the Bible Reading and Prayer, and then end it with the Reflection. Or, if you're more of a doer, you might want to focus on the Do section, and maybe read the Bible reading over a cuppa as and when you can.

For those of you who like to spend more time in your Bible, there is a daily Dive Deeper section, with Bible passages linked to the reading for that day. And if you find God in art, you might find the hand drawn illustrations a helpful meditative aid, or you might even wish to create your own daily drawings to hang on a Jesse tree during advent.

For me, it's a pick and mix approach. It depends on what the day is like, how the children are, and how I'm feeling – one day I might be able to enjoy every part, whereas the next will find me struggling to squeeze a three-minute prayer in. But however you enjoy this devotional, I pray that it may be a book which equips you as saints for the work of ministry.

just as new
branches sprout
from a stump,
so a new
King will
arise

DAY
ONE

DEVOTIONAL

The Jesse Tree

Have you ever been for a walk in the woods, and come across a tree stump? Maybe you've counted the lines, or even climbed up onto it. Compared to the other trees, they're quite small, aren't they?

Years ago, a King called David had a son named Solomon, and although Solomon was known for his wisdom, he made some bad choices – and this meant that the kingdom got smaller, broken into pieces like a rotten tree stump.

But there's good news. It's not broken forever! This messenger of God, Isaiah, encourages God's people that one day, a healthy big tree will grow from this stump once again. He is talking about Jesus, coming down to be with us and restore us.

So next time you're in the woods and playing on a stump, remember how God loved us so much that he came as Jesus, to transform God's people from a mouldy stump to a strong, towering tree.

DIVE DEEPER
Luke 3:32
Romans 15:12

BIBLE PASSAGE

Isaiah 11:1-2
The royal line of David is like a tree that has been cut down; but just as new branches sprout from a stump, so a new king will arise from among David's descendants. The Spirit of the Lord will give him wisdom and the knowledge and skill to rule his people. He will know the Lord's will and honour him.

PRAY

Jesus, thank you that you can bring amazing things out of stuff that seems small or broken. Help us to bring hope to people who feel a bit like a small stump, and please bring new life in the name of Jesus. Amen.

THINK

Is there a part of your life that you think is too small for God to do anything with? Perhaps you yourself think of yourself as more like a shoot than a tree?

DO

Pop outside – what's the biggest, longest stick you can find? Now, what about the smallest? Put it somewhere in your house to remind you that God can make amazing things out of small stumps.

TAKE NOTE...

_____

_____

_____

_____

_____

_____

_____

_____

_____

_____

_____

_____

_____

_____

_____

_____

_____

'GOD Looked AT everthing HE HAD made, HE WAS VERY pleased'

___

DAY
TWO

BIBLE PASSAGE

Genesis 1:25-27, 31
So God made them all, and he was pleased with what he saw.
Then God said, "And now we will make human beings; they will be like us and resemble us. They will have power over the fish, the birds, and all animals, domestic and wild, large and small." So God created human beings, making them to be like himself.

God looked at everything he had made, and he was very pleased. Evening passed and morning came; that was the sixth day.

DIVE
DEEPER
Psalm 8:4-8
Hebrews 2:6-9

DEVOTIONAL

Creation of Humans
Do you like making things? Maybe you like baking cupcakes, building towers, or playing with playdough?
God likes to create, too. And today we read that, at the beginning of time, God made the universe – the moon, stars, planets, animals – and even us! Wow. And when he made us all, he looked and was really pleased. He even said it was very good. And for God to say something is very good, it must be very good! And when God made creation, he made us to be in a relationship with him. To be close with him, to talk with him, to walk with him, and to enjoy all that he had made. Next time you're making something – maybe some work at school, or something crafty at home – remember that God made you, and thinks you are amazing! God loves you.

PRAY

God, thank you for your creation. Thank you for your wisdom and creativity, and thank you that you made me. Amen.

THINK

What was the last thing you made? How did you feel when you made it – both during its creation, and then afterwards?

DO

Why don't you have a go at making something? You might spend hours baking an amazing, delicious cake – or a few minutes crafting a zooming, soaring paper aeroplane. As you make it, think about how God made you, and knows you – WOW!

RECORD YOUR CREATIONS...

But the Lord God
called out to the man,

"Where
are
you?"

DAY
THREE

BIBLE PASSAGE

Genesis 3:8-13

That evening they heard the Lord God walking in the garden, and they hid from him among the trees. But the Lord God called out to the man, "Where are you?" He answered, "I heard you in the garden; I was afraid and hid from you, because I was naked."

"Who told you that you were naked?" God asked. "Did you eat the fruit that I told you not to eat?" The man answered, "The woman you put here with me gave me the fruit, and I ate it." The Lord God asked the woman, "Why did you do this?" She replied, "The snake tricked me into eating it."

DEVOTIONAL

The Fall

Have you ever been tricked by someone? Maybe there was a time when you weren't entirely truthful, and it made someone else sad?

In this reading, we hear about how Adam and Eve make a bad choice. Instead of listening to God, they decide to go against him and eat fruit from the tree God asks them to avoid. They have a choice – but they choose the wrong way.

There's good news, though! God loves us even when we make wrong choices. And he showed that love in the most incredible way when he came to earth as a human to live among us.

DIVE DEEPER

Jeremiah 23:24
Romans 5:12 - end

PRAY

God, I'm sorry for when I've made the wrong choices, and not listened to you. Thank you that you forgive my mistakes. Help me to listen to you more, and follow your words. Amen.

THINK

Have you ever made a choice that you knew, deep down, was wrong? (I know I have!) Why did you make that choice? What happened afterwards?

DO

See if you can find a piece of fruit. Pick it up and hold it in your hand – how does it feel? Is it smooth or rough, warm or cool? Hold it for a while and think about it, then put it back, and as you do so, ask God to help you listen to him. Then rest for a moment in his hands.

If you can't find a piece of fruit, reflect on a picture of your favourite fruit and think about how it would feel, smell and taste, and ask God to speak to you as you imagine.

DRAW ROUND YOUR HAND,
WRITE & DRAW YOUR PRAYERS.

"*it will be the sign of my covenant with the world*"

_____

DAY
FOUR

BIBLE PASSAGE

Genesis 9:11-13

With these words I make my covenant with you: I promise that never again will all living beings be destroyed by a flood; never again will a flood destroy the earth. As a sign of this everlasting covenant which I am making with you and with all living beings, I am putting my bow in the clouds. It will be the sign of my covenant with the world."

DEVOTIONAL

Noah's Ark

In 2020, many people displayed rainbows in their windows as a thank you to our wonderful NHS during the pandemic. But thousands of years ago, God used a rainbow as a symbol of something even more wonderful – to remind us that there would never again be a great flood to renew the world, to remind us that he is a God who keeps promises.

Instead of the world being once again consumed by water, and many living things dying, God the Son himself died for us. Jesus, consumed by death and buried in a tomb, was raised to life and broke the power of death. And so, whenever we see a rainbow, we can thank God for his love and faithfulness. We can thank him for his amazing grace and loving patience, that even when we mess up he still loves us, still forgives us when we turn to him.

DIVE DEEPER
Hebrews 11:7
1 Peter 3:20

PRAY

God, we know we live in a world where some people do bad things. But thank you for your patience. Thank you that you came to earth as a human just like us, that you died and then rose to life, so that all the messes we make can be forgiven and we can be free. Amen.

THINK

Why do you think Noah's Ark is such a popular children story, and what is it about the narrative that makes it such a compelling tale? Can you think of any other events in the Bible that draw you in like this one?

DO

Why not make your own rainbow? It could be a quick thing done with some paints, or a painstaking 3d work of art – create it however you'd like. And display it somewhere to remind you of God's everlasting promise of love and forgiveness.

MAKE YOUR OWN RAINBOW HERE!

this is the
COUNTRY
that i am
going to
give to your
DESCENDANTS

——————

DAY
FIVE

BIBLE PASSAGE

Genesis 12:1-3
The Lord said to Abram, "Leave your country, your relatives, and your father's home, and go to a land that I am going to show you. I will give you many descendants, and they will become a great nation. I will bless you and make your name famous, so that you will be a blessing.
I will bless those who bless you, But I will curse those who curse you. And through you I will bless all the nations."

DIVE DEEPER
Hebrews 12:1-3
Joshua 5:6

DEVOTIONAL

The Promised Land
Have you ever been on a really long walk? Maybe you've taken some food with you in a rucksack, put some good shoes on, and gone out for a few hours. Or what about a long car journey? Or even a holiday?

There's something exciting about travelling, isn't there? It's fun to stay in new places. But it's always nice to come home, too. Today we journey with Abram, who left everything he knew to follow God to a new land full of promise.

How do you think Abram felt? He must have been sad to leave all that he knew behind – but excited, all at the same time, to be journeying to a new place with God. When God calls us to new things and new places, we too can travel with excitement, knowing God is with us all the way.

Think about how God speaks to Abram about how his descendants will become a blessing, and how his words point forward to Jesus – one of those descendants – the one by whom all nations are blessed.

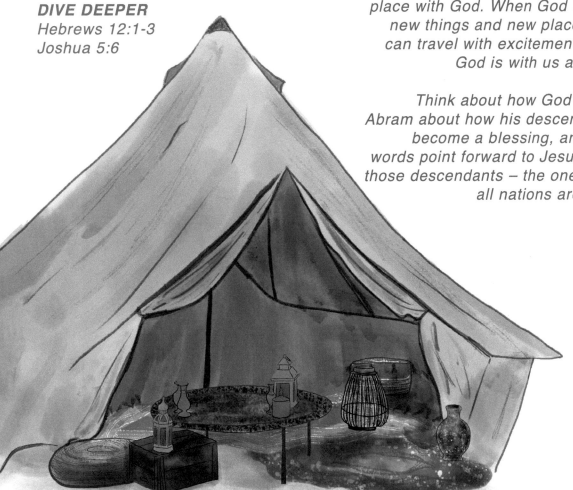

PRAY

God, thank you that you are always with us, even when we find ourselves in new places and doing new things. Help us to trust you – and thank you for Jesus, through whom all the nations can be blessed.

DO

Go for a walk. Maybe a familiar one, where your feet know where they are going, or maybe just see where your legs want to take you.
Take a flask of coffee, and a Bible, and see where you end up, and what God teaches you.

THINK

What is your most memorable journey? What might God have been teaching you on the way?

TAKE NOTE...

"Do not be afraid,
Abram. I will shield you
from danger & give you
great reward."

**DAY
SIX**

BIBLE PASSAGE

Genesis 15:1, 5-6
After this, Abram had a vision and heard the Lord say to him, "Do not be afraid, Abram. I will shield you from danger and give you a great reward."

The Lord took him outside and said, "Look at the sky and try to count the stars; you will have as many descendants as that."
Abram put his trust in the Lord, and because of this the Lord was pleased with him and accepted him.

DEVOTIONAL

God's Promise to Abraham
On a clear dark night, when the sky is inky black, there's nothing quite like lying on a blanket and gazing up at the stars. Once your eyes are tuned in, you spot more and more stars splashed across the heavens. It's glorious.

Today, we learn that God tells Abram not to be afraid – and promises that his family will be as numerous as the stars in the sky. And if you have ever looked into the night sky, you will have an inkling of just how many that would be.

You see, those of us who follow Jesus are descendants of Abraham – who put his trust in the Lord.

Isn't it amazing that the God who made the stars, and knows each one, also knows and loves us? What is he calling you to trust in him about today?

DIVE DEEPER
Ephesians 1:4-5
Genesis 16:1-2

(for an insight into a time when Abraham didn't quite trust as well as he should!)

PRAY

Father God, thank you that you are the creator of all the millions of stars that sparkle in the night sky, but that you also made me and love me. Help me to trust in you, just as Abram did. Amen.

DO

Go for a walk and find a pebble you love the look of. Maybe you might like to paint a picture of the moon and stars on it. When it's dry, put it into your pocket and through the day keep touching it and holding it in your hand, allowing it to be a constant reminder that although you are tiny, God knows you well and is thinking about you all the time.

THINK

Can you think of a time you felt really, really small? Maybe you were looking into the sky at night, or bobbing on a small boat in the ocean, or gazing up at a lofty skyscraper – how did you feel? Hold that feeling, and thank God that he knows and loves you.

WHEN DID YOU NOTICE GOD TODAY?

"On the Lord's mountain he provides."

DAY
SEVEN

BIBLE PASSAGE

Genesis 22:1-2, 6-14

Some time later God tested Abraham; he called to him, "Abraham!" And Abraham answered, "Yes, here I am!"
"Take your son," God said, "your only son, Isaac, whom you love so much, and go to the land of Moriah. There on a mountain that I will show you, offer him as a sacrifice to me."

Abraham made Isaac carry the wood for the sacrifice, and he himself carried a knife and live coals for starting the fire. As they walked along together, Isaac spoke up, "Father!"
He answered, "Yes, my son?"
Isaac asked, "I see that you have the coals and the wood, but where is the lamb for the sacrifice?"
Abraham answered, "God himself will provide one." And the two of them walked on together.

When they came to the place which God had told him about, Abraham built an altar and arranged the wood on it. He tied up his son and placed him on the altar, on top of the wood. Then he picked up the knife to kill him. But the angel of the Lord called to him from heaven, "Abraham, Abraham!"
He answered, "Yes, here I am."
"Don't hurt the boy or do anything to him," he said. "Now I know that you honour and obey God, because you have not kept back your only son from him."

Abraham looked around and saw a ram caught in a bush by its horns. He went and got it and offered it as a burnt offering instead of his son. Abraham named that place "The Lord Provides." And even today people say, "On the Lord's mountain he provides."

DEVOTIONAL

Abraham and Isaac

There are lots of stories in the Old Testament which point to Jesus – they give us a hint of the coming Messiah. And when we read them through the 'lens' of knowing who Jesus is and what he has done, we gain a greater insight into these passages of Scripture:

A son given as sacrifice.

That son carrying the heavy load of wood on his back up the hill.

A ram, caught in thorn – and later Jesus, the lamb of God, found himself wearing a crown of thorns as he went to the cross.

This story can make us feel a little uneasy and uncomfortable. Maybe it seems a bit unfair, or even cruel, of God, to demand that Abraham be willing to sacrifice his son. Tempting as it is to skim over the bits which make us uncomfortable, it's actually good to reflect on parts of the Bible we don't like, and ask God what he's saying through them to us.

Isaac's dad trusted in God, even when stuff looked bad. He trusted God, even though he didn't really understand, and, right at the last minute, God provided the ram for the sacrifice. God didn't really want Isaac to be sacrificed after all, he just wanted his dad to keep trusting in him. Many years later, God became a sacrifice for us, because of his great love.

We can trust our God of hope to provide what we need. Even when we are struggling up a hill with a heavy load, we know God is walking beside us, catching us when we stumble.

PRAY

Dear Jesus. thank you that you came to Earth to become the sacrifice on the cross for the wrongs we do – that you were the lamb with the crown of thorns. Help us to honour you, and your sacrifice, in our lives, and to trust you, even when the going is tough. Amen.

THINK

Have you ever felt like Abraham must have done; that God has asked you something impossible? What was your response? What would God's full provision look like in your life today?

DO

Find a hill nearby, and have a wander up it. You might even be able to carry some sticks as you go. How does the wood feel in your hands? And how does the view of the area all around you change as you climb? Or maybe you could make a big hill out of cushions, or some sand or mud, or even a pile of laundry, then place a favourite toy, photo or item on the top. Think about how it would feel to leave it there.

DIVE DEEPER
Hebrews 11:17
John 8:39

DRAW THE VIEW HERE!

"The Lord is here!
He is in this place,
and I didn't know it!"

DAY
EIGHT

BIBLE PASSAGE

Genesis 28:10-17

Jacob left Beersheba and started toward Haran. At sunset he came to a holy place and camped there. He lay down to sleep, resting his head on a stone. He dreamed that he saw a stairway reaching from earth to heaven, with angels going up and coming down on it. And there was the Lord standing beside him. "I am the Lord, the God of Abraham and Isaac," he said. "I will give to you and to your descendants this land on which you are lying. They will be as numerous as the specks of dust on the earth. They will extend their territory in all directions, and through you and your descendants I will bless all the nations. Remember, I will be with you and protect you wherever you go, and I will bring you back to this land. I will not leave you until I have done all that I have promised you."

Jacob woke up and said, "The Lord is here! He is in this place, and I didn't know it!" He was afraid and said, "What a terrifying place this is! It must be the house of God; it must be the gate that opens into heaven."

DEVOTIONAL

Jacob's Dream

Have you ever had a strange dream? What is the weirdest dream that you can remember?

Today, we read about Jacob's weird dream. A dream about a ladder and a load of angels is pretty out there! Yet God speaks to him through this dream, reminding him that he will always be with him, and always keep him safe.

God knew that Jacob might be a bit worried, but wanted to remind him that he would always be there for him. Isn't it good to know that, even when we sleep, God watches over us – and, like Jacob, he will always be with us. He keeps his promises!

And remember – next time you have a dream, be open to God speaking to you through it...

PRAY

God, thank you that you will always be with us, and that you are faithful. Whenever we are worried, or weary, help us to trust in your promises.

THINK

What was the last dream you had? What can you remember about it, and how did it make you feel? What might God have been teaching you through it?

DO

Keep a notebook and pen by your bed, and if you remember a dream when you wake up, jot it down. If you're an energetic type, why not go for some playful silliness and do some (supervised!) racing up and down the stairs? As you're recovering your breath, have a ponder about what on earth (and off it!) these angels were up to...

WHAT WAS YOUR LAST DREAM?

Joseph
SAID, "I AM
READY."

DAY
NINE

BIBLE PASSAGE

Genesis 37:12, 18-27
One day when Joseph's brothers had gone to Shechem to take care of their father's flock.

They saw him in the distance, and before he reached them, they plotted against him and decided to kill him. They said to one another, "Here comes that dreamer. Come on now, let's kill him and throw his body into one of the dry wells. We can say that a wild animal killed him. Then we will see what becomes of his dreams."

When Joseph came up to his brothers, they ripped off his long robe with full sleeves. Then they took him and threw him into the well, which was dry.

While they were eating, they suddenly saw a group of Ishmaelites traveling from Gilead to Egypt. Their camels were loaded with spices and resins. Judah said to his brothers, "What will we gain by killing our brother and covering up the murder? Let's sell him to these Ishmaelites. Then we won't have to hurt him; after all, he is our brother, our own flesh and blood."

DEVOTIONAL

Coat of many colours

*Who can read this story without bursting into song?
'I wore my coat...I wore my coat...ahahaaaa...'*

*This classic story has been brought to life as a
Broadway phenomenon, as well as in numerous
plays, books and films. We are gripped by this story
of a band of brothers who hate the youngest of
them all, and so try to rid themselves of him, getting
him sold into slavery in Egypt. We are caught up in
the narrative as Joseph becomes Pharaoh's
right-hand man, partnering with God to warn the
nation about an upcoming famine, and helping to
prepare enough food to keep the country fed and
watered.*

*When Joseph's brothers come looking for food, they
don't even recognize him. But he does something
incredible: he gives them food – and more than that
– he forgives them. He tells them that even though
they had intended him harm, God used it for good.*

PRAY

God, thank you that you are not limited by our sin. When we make bad choices, you are still working for good. Help us to follow you more closely, to love people more deeply, and to see your kingdom come more powerfully. Amen.

THINK

What a rollercoaster ride Joseph went on! Have a read of his whole story in Genesis 37-50, thinking about how he must have felt – from the lows of betrayal through to the highs of his new place as second-in-command. How would you have felt, and responded? Which parts of the story most resonate with where you are with God right now, and why?

DO

Put on the most colourful outfit you can find. It doesn't have to match, and you don't have to post it on social media – although I'd love to see it! Then why not spend a little time blasting out your favourite worship song, boogieing along in your funky attire, thanking God that he is always working for good!

CAN YOU THINK OF A MOMENT TODAY WHEN
YOU WERE AWARE OF GOD?

DAY
TEN

DEVOTIONAL

The 10 Commandments

I wonder how good you are at sticking to rules? At school, home, and work, there are rules for grown-ups and children alike! For example, when I drive my car, I'm not allowed to go over a certain speed, and I have to keep to the left-hand side of the road.

Rules can seem like a drag, but they keep us safe. Today we read of how God gives his people the ten commandments, which are rules to keep them safe, and to help them live their lives as well as pos sible.

These rules are life-giving, and they include:
- *Only worship God*
- *Take time to rest*

Don't be jealous of what other people have.

Sometimes we might think that rules are there to stop us having any fun. But the strange thing with God's rules is that, actually, when we follow them, we find that our life is more amazing than it could ever be without them.

BIBLE PASSAGE

Deuteronomy 5:6-21

'I am the Lord your God, who rescued you from Egypt, where you were slaves.
"Worship no god but me.

"Do not make for yourselves images of anything in heaven or on earth or in the water under the earth...

"Do not use my name for evil purposes, for I, the Lord your God, will punish anyone who misuses my name.

"Observe the Sabbath and keep it holy, as I, the Lord your God, have commanded you...

"Respect your father and your mother...

"Do not commit murder.

"Do not commit adultery.

"Do not steal.

"Do not accuse anyone falsely.

"Do not desire another man's wife; do not desire his house, his land, his slaves, his cattle, his donkeys, or anything else that he owns.'

DIVE DEEPER
Matthew 19:16-29
Romans 7:14

PRAY

God, thank you for loving us enough that you want to keep us safe and help us live the best that we can. Help us to keep these commandments, that we might enjoy life, and life in all its full-ness. Amen.

THINK

Are you a natural rule keeper, or rule breaker? How do you feel when you get caught breaking rules- are you naturally an apologizer, or a defender? As you read through the 10 commandments, which ones jump out at you? Do you find some more difficult than others?

DO

The 10 Commandments were carved into tablets of stone. Find a piece of wood, or a pebble, or some playdough, and have a go at carving an arrow into it. Or you could use some chalk on a chalkboard. Then place it somewhere you will see it every-day, as a reminder that you want to keep going forward with Jesus.

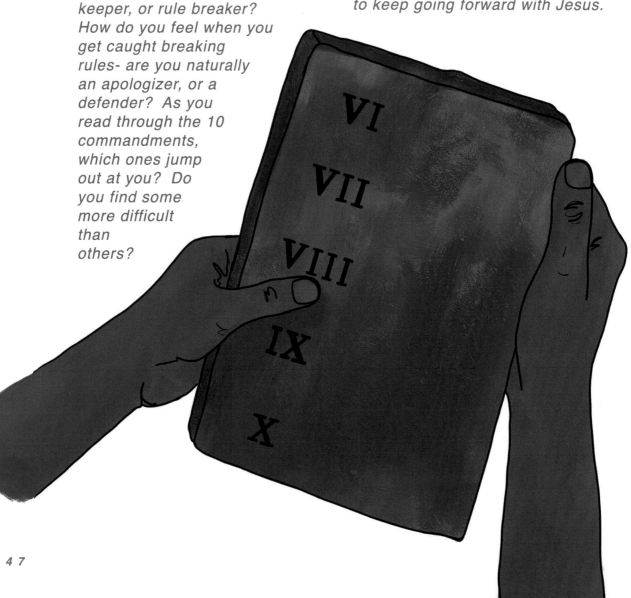

WHERE DO YOU WANT TO SEE JESUS?

THE
LORD YOUR
GOD
IS GOD IN
HEAVEN
ABOVE
&
HERE ON
EARTH

DAY
ELEVEN

BIBLE PASSAGE

Joshua 2:1, 8-18, 21

Then Joshua sent two spies from the camp at Acacia with orders to go and secretly explore the land of Canaan, especially the city of Jericho. When they came to the city, they went to spend the night in the house of a prostitute named Rahab.

Before the spies settled down for the night, Rahab went up on the roof and said to them, "I know that the Lord has given you this land. Everyone in the country is terrified of you...

Promise me that you will save my father and mother, my brothers and sisters, and all their families! Don't let us be killed!"

The men said to her, "May God take our lives if we don't do as we say! If you do not tell anyone what we have been doing, we promise you that when the Lord gives us this land, we will treat you well."

Rahab lived in a house built into the city wall, so she let the men down from the window by a rope. "Go into the hill country," she said, "or the king's men will find you. Hide there for three days until they come back. After that, you can go on your way."

The men said to her, "We will keep the promise that you have made us give. This is what you must do. When we invade your land, tie this red cord to the window you let us down from."
She agreed and sent them away. When they had gone, she tied the red cord to the window.

DIVE DEEPER
Hebrews 11:31
Matthew 1:5

DEVOTIONAL

Rahab

What a story! Adventure, spies, exploration, daring escapes... sounds like something out of a Hollywood blockbuster, doesn't it?

Two spies from Israel are secretly checking out a city, Jericho, but they know that it's full of danger, and they're scared. But there's a lady there who has heard of all the amazing things God has done, and she hides the spies, keeping them safe in her home, then helping them escape. She knows the king of her city wants to find them, and she could get in huge trouble, but she helps them anyway. Her name is Rahab.

Rahab must feel scared of the king, and what he might do, but she's also scared of not doing the right thing for the God she's heard about, and his two spies. She must feel very mixed up!

Of course, this story has a great ending, because the spies pull off their great escape, and Rahab's family are protected when the city is attacked. And, to top it all, Rahab's name is added to Jesus' family tree, because of her faith and courage.

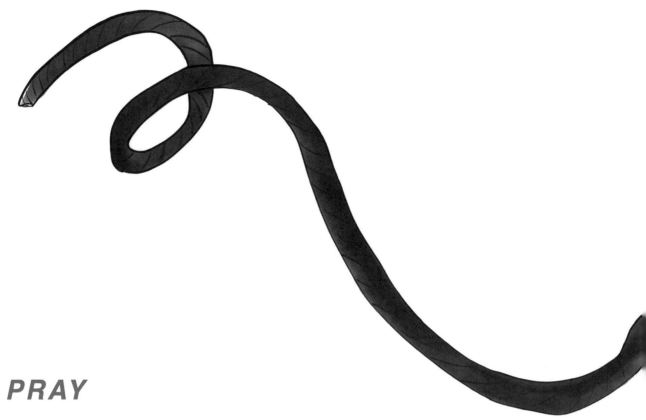

PRAY

Lord, when we are torn between two things, help us to choose to do the right one. And thank you that, in the same way that both the spies and Rahab were rescued from danger, so you have brought us out of the darkness into your marvellous light.

THINK

How do you think Rahab would have felt? Have you ever been in a situation where you've felt torn between two fairly scary things? What might it look like in your present situation to see God help you escape from that fear?

DO

Have a go at doing something today which scares you a little bit! This could be holding a creepy-crawly, smiling at a stranger, or even offering to pray for someone. Step out, like Rahab.

USE THIS SPACE TO WRITE & DRAW YOUR
THOUGHTS & PRAYERS.

may the lord
reward you
for what you
have done.

DAY
TWELVE

BIBLE PASSAGE

Ruth 2:1-3, 8-12
Naomi had a relative named Boaz, a rich and influential man who belonged to the family of her husband Elimelech. One day Ruth said to Naomi, "Let me go to the fields to gather the grain that the harvest workers leave. I am sure to find someone who will let me work with him."

Naomi answered, "Go ahead, daughter."

So Ruth went out to the fields and walked behind the workers, picking up the heads of grain which they left. It so happened that she was in a field that belonged to Boaz.

Then Boaz said to Ruth, "Let me give you some advice. Don't gather grain anywhere except in this field. Work with the women here; watch them to see where they are reaping and stay with them. I have ordered my men not to molest you. And whenever you are thirsty, go and drink from the water jars that they have filled."

Ruth bowed down with her face touching the ground, and said to Boaz, "Why should you be so concerned about me? Why should you be so kind to a foreigner?"

Boaz answered, "I have heard about everything that you have done for your mother-in-law since your husband died. I know how you left your father and mother and your own country and how you came to live among a people you had never known before. May the Lord reward you for what you have done. May you have a full reward from the Lord God of Israel, to whom you have come for protection!"

DEVOTIONAL

Ruth and Boaz

Was I the only one at school who was often one of the last standing, waiting to be picked for a team? So often, we feel as if we just don't fit in, especially when we're playing a game where everyone else is better than us, or when our friends are chatting about something we don't know much about.

Ruth might have felt a bit like that too, sometimes. She must have felt different when she moved to a strange land with her mother-in-law, Naomi, a land that was foreign to her. But when she married Boaz, he made her feel welcome and at home, because he looked after her, and they were happy together. They had a son, who would one day be the grandad of King David. So Ruth was King David's great-grandma!

And one day, another baby would be born into that same family line. A baby named Jesus, a descendant of David. So Ruth, the woman who felt an outsider, found herself right there on Jesus' family tree!

DIVE DEEPER
Luke 3:32
Romans 9:24-26

PRAY

Thank you, Jesus, that all are welcome in your family. Help us to follow you like Ruth did, even when we might find it hard. Amen.

THINK

Have you ever been in a situation where you have felt like an outsider? How did it feel to not fit in? Did anyone say anything to you or come alongside you to help you feel included?

DO

Pray for someone you know who might feel like they are an outsider. How can you help them to feel included and welcome today? Maybe you could drop them a text, or bake them a cake, or take them a coffee, or even deliver a surprise gift to their home.

HOW CAN YOU HELP SOMEONE TODAY?

and
HE WILL
bring
PEACE

DAY
THIRTEEN

BIBLE PASSAGE

1 Samuel 16:1, 6-12

The Lord said to Samuel, "How long will you go on grieving over Saul? I have rejected him as king of Israel. But now get some olive oil and go to Bethlehem, to a man named Jesse, because I have chosen one of his sons to be king."

When they arrived, Samuel saw Jesse's son Eliab and said to himself, "This man standing here in the Lord's presence is surely the one he has chosen." But the Lord said to him, "Pay no attention to how tall and handsome he is. I have rejected him, because I do not judge as people judge. They look at the outward appearance, but I look at the heart."

Then Jesse called his son Abinadab and brought him to Samuel. But Samuel said, "No, the Lord hasn't chosen him either." Jesse then brought Shammah. "No, the Lord hasn't chosen him either," Samuel said. In this way Jesse brought seven of his sons to Samuel. And Samuel said to him, "No, the Lord hasn't chosen any of these." Then he asked him, "Do you have any more sons?"

Jesse answered, "There is still the youngest, but he is out taking care of the sheep."

"Tell him to come here," Samuel said. "We won't offer the sacrifice until he comes." So Jesse sent for him. He was a handsome, healthy young man, and his eyes sparkled. The Lord said to Samuel, "This is the one—anoint him!"

DIVE DEEPER
Acts 13:21-22
Psalm 78:70

DEVOTIONAL

God chooses David

What do you think a King should be like? Strong? Courageous? Wise? Rich? Powerful? When you watch a movie about a king, those are some of the attributes you'll probably see. Think about Thor, for example – in that film, Prince Thor is certain that in order to be a strong king, he must wage war and conquer his enemies. He must be stronger and bigger than anyone else.

But today's reading turns that story upside down. Instead of going for the biggest and strongest, God chooses Jesse's youngest, smallest son to be the King of Israel. (Remember how we thought about how a tiny shoot grows out of a tree on Day One?) And this smallest son, David, although he was only a kid looking after the sheep, was picked for a great purpose.

You see, people so often look at what a person looks like on the outside – but God always looks at the heart.

LET'S PRAY

Thank you God that we don't have to be the biggest, or strongest, loudest or oldest to be chosen by you. In fact, we're all chosen! So help us to bring you glory every day. Amen.

THINK

What films have you seen that feature a king? What was he like? Do you think he was a great king, or was he a bit rubbish? Think about what made him good or bad or in-between, and whether all kings are like the ones in the movies.

DO

How small can you make yourself? Curl yourself up in a small ball. Now, slowly uncurl whilst standing up – how big and tall can you make yourself? Why don't you listen to or sing the song 'Big Family of God' by Nick and Becky Drake to remind yourself that God chooses you, whatever you look like and whoever you are, even if you are the smallest.

THEY WILL BE SAVED

DAY
FOURTEEN

BIBLE PASSAGE

Esther 4:12-16

When Mordecai received Esther's message, he sent her this warning: "Don't imagine that you are safer than any other Jew just because you are in the royal palace. If you keep quiet at a time like this, help will come from heaven to the Jews, and they will be saved, but you will die and your father's family will come to an end. Yet who knows—maybe it was for a time like this that you were made queen!"
Esther sent Mordecai this reply: "Go and get all the Jews in Susa together; hold a fast and pray for me. Don't eat or drink anything for three days and nights. My servant women and I will be doing the same. After that, I will go to the king, even though it is against the law. If I must die for doing it, I will die."

DIVE DEEPER
Ephesians 6:10
Acts 4:29-37

DEVOTIONAL

Esther Saves her people

God isn't actually mentioned by name in the book of Esther, but he is very clearly at work. It could be said that, although God's name doesn't appear, his fingerprints are all over the place.

We tremble with Queen Esther as she prepares to present herself to the king without being sent for, knowing that could mean big trouble for her. A tiny bit like you just wandering into your headteacher's office at school without even knocking – only a million times worse.

Esther is sure of what she has to do, and even though it's scary, she goes for it anyway. She asks the king to spare all her people, who are at risk of being killed. And he does as she asks! (God's finger-prints again...) He makes a law to keep them safe. Because of Esther's bravery, all the Jews in the kingdom are saved. When we're a bit worried about something that God is asking us to do, isn't it great that God is always with us!

LET'S PRAY

God, thank you for Esther's bravery. Will you fill us with the same kind of courage when you call us to speak out against injustice, on behalf of the vulnerable, or to speak out the words you inspire us to say. Amen.

THINK

Have you ever needed to be really brave about something that you felt God was asking you to do or say? Read through Esther's story and think about which parts speak to you the most. Why do you think God isn't explicitly named in this story?

Think about how God's fingerprints are on your story, too, even through scary situations. What might you need courage for today? What do you think that courage will look like?

DO

Esther spoke up for the vulnerable, as we are called to do. Find a charity or organization which supports people who are defenseless, and pledge to support them. You could pray for them weekly, help financially, or lobby the government for their cause.

YOU HAVE GIVEN THEM GREAT JOY

DAY
FIFTEEN

BIBLE PASSAGE

Isaiah 9:2-3, 6-7

The people who walked in darkness have seen a great light. They lived in a land of shadows, but now light is shining on them. You have given them great joy, Lord; you have made them happy. They rejoice in what you have done, as people rejoice when they harvest grain or when they divide captured wealth.

A child is born to us! A son is given to us! And he will be our ruler. He will be called, "Wonderful Counselor," "Mighty God," "Eternal Father," "Prince of Peace." His royal power will continue to grow; his kingdom will always be at peace. He will rule as King David's successor, basing his power on right and justice, from now until the end of time. The Lord Almighty is determined to do all this.

DIVE DEEPER
1 Peter 2:9
Matthew 4:16

DEVOTIONAL

Isaiah's prophecy of a Saviour

Have you ever experienced a power cut, where all the lights go off and none of your electrical appliances will work – even the TV? What's the first thing you do? If you're anything like me, you hunt out a torch, or find a candle and some matches. It's not easy to do anything when you're floundering in the dark, is it?

In this reading, Isaiah is talking to people who have walked in the darkness for a very long time – not physically, but spiritually. They have been floundering around in the dark, lost and alone, unable to see their way out. They've been living in this land of shadows so long that they have probably forgotten what light looks like, and where they were going. But Isaiah is here to give them some great news: the light is coming...

Jesus is the great light shining on them – he will be called wonderful, counsellor, mighty God. And he will bring bright light to dark places. Good news!

LET'S PRAY

Thank you, Jesus, that you flood our darkness with your light. We pray for those people we know who are floundering in the dark, who cannot see the path ahead of them, and ask that you will shine your glorious light on them and bring them into freedom. Amen.

THINK

How do you feel in the dark? Safe? Lonely? Worried? Peaceful? Perhaps you react differently, depending on where the darkness is and where you are.
Have another look at verses 4 and 5, and think about how a new and great light would change the feelings of those who are lost in deep darkness.

DO

Create an indoor obstacle course. Time yourself to see how long it takes you to complete the course. Then switch off the lights, close the curtains and blindfold yourself – and try it again! (Don't forget to have an adult with you!)
How much more difficult did you find it when it was dark? Thank God for his glorious light, which pierces through all the darkness.

WHAT ARE YOU GRATEFUL FOR?

the land
will be full
of knowledge
the lord
as the seas
are full of
water

DAY
SIXTEEN

BIBLE PASSAGE

DEVOTIONAL

Isaiah 11:6-9

Wolves and sheep will live together in peace, and leopards will lie down with young goats. Calves and lion cubs will feed together, and little children will take care of them. Cows and bears will eat together, and their calves and cubs will lie down in peace. Lions will eat straw as cattle do. Even a baby will not be harmed if it plays near a poisonous snake. On Zion, God's sacred hill, there will be nothing harmful or evil. The land will be as full of knowledge of the Lord as the seas are full of water.

DIVE DEEPER
Hosea 2:18
Micah 4:2-4

Isaiah's prophecy of the second coming.

Have you ever seen the clip from a wildlife documentary – showing a terrified lizard's tense escape from a gang of very hungry snakes – which went viral on the internet? As the lizard scuttled across the ground, the snakes did their best to snatch him away from freedom and into their snarling clutches. But he made it out of there, and the world breathed a sigh of relief. If you haven't seen it, google it at your own risk!

In today's reading, we're given a vivid picture of a wolf and sheep lying down together, alongside leopards and goats, cows and bears, and other unlikely pairings. Think about what it would be like if the snakes in that video simply snuggled down with that lizard and they all fell asleep, to give you an idea of the strangeness of Isaiah's image – a reversal of nature's 'normal'!

One day, Jesus will return, and then the whole world will be at peace. No more attacks on one another. No more conflict, or hatred, or fear. Just like these animals who are at peace in one another's company, we too will at last be at peace with one another – an astounding, profound peace. Nothing will be able to harm us anymore. Can you imagine?

PRAY

Thank you, Jesus, that you are going to return, and bring peace we cannot understand. Fill us with yearning hope for that day, and, while we are waiting, help us to speak of your peace to others, and to walk in your peace every day of our lives. Amen.

THINK

What would a world truly at peace look like? What would be different? How different would our lives be if we had peace with others? What could you do to be a peacemaker today?

DO

Jesus told us to pray for our enemies and those who persecute us, in anticipation of the peace he will bring to the earth. Think about the people you find difficult, those who make life hard for you, and have a think about how you could be kind to them today. You could pray for them, and you could also do something for them to show you care, like baking them a cake or sending them a message. See what God does when you follow his commands!

GOD SAYS THAT WE SHOULD
PRAY FOR OUR ENEMIES

go to Nineveh,
that great city,
& proclaim
to the people
the message I
have given you

———————

DAY
SEVENTEEN

BIBLE PASSAGE

Jonah 3:1-5

Once again the Lord spoke to Jonah. He said, "Go to Nineveh, that great city, and proclaim to the people the message I have given you." So Jonah obeyed the Lord and went to Nineveh, a city so large that it took three days to walk through it. Jonah started through the city, and after walking a whole day, he proclaimed, "In forty days Nineveh will be destroyed!"
The people of Nineveh believed God's message. So they decided that everyone should fast, and all the people, from the greatest to the least, put on sackcloth to show that they had repented.

DEVOTIONAL

Jonah and the Fish

God asks Jonah to travel to the city of Nineveh to tell the people who live there all about him. But Jonah gets scared, running away instead. He runs so far he ends up on a boat in the middle of a storm, and then right in the belly of a very big fish!

The fish gets a bit tired of Jonah and spits him out (yuck!) on a beach near to the city God wanted Jonah to visit in the first place. Jonah decides he'd better go, after all, to tell the people of the city to turn to God – and God works through Jonah to turn the people's hearts to him. Sometimes we might feel scared of something God is asking us to do. Maybe we don't feel we are good enough, clever enough or strong enough. Perhaps we might think it's a daft idea, and so we want to turn away. Jonah did, after all, but his story shows us that God's ways are always good, and we should listen when he speaks to us. We can also see that God gives us more chances when we mess up! He never turns his back on us.

DIVE DEEPER
Matthew 12:41
John 5:19

PRAY

Dear God, help us to hear your voice, and fill us with courage to do what you ask of us, whether you call us to pray for someone or invite a friend to church, or inspire us to any other action. Help us to stay close to you, rather than running away, even when it feels too tough. Amen.

THINK

Think about what strikes you most as you read this passage, and why. Then reflect for a while on what your 'Nineveh' is, right now – what is God calling you to? Where do you find yourself in relation to this call? Are you on the boat, or sinking into the waves, or in the belly of the fish? Maybe you're washed up on shore, or sitting under the shade of a tree – what are you going to do next?

DO

Find some paper, paint, and a straw, and very carefully begin to suck the paint through the straw – but don't let it get as far as your mouth! Then give it a 'puff', just like the fish puffed out Jonah. Keep repeating with different colours, and see what a fabulous picture you can create. (If you'd rather not get so messy, just blow some bubbles in a glass of water). Once your wonderful artwork is finished and dried out, stick it up somewhere as a reminder to say Yes to God.

SAY YES TO GOD!

May your God,
whom you serve so
loyally, rescue you.

———————

DAY
EIGHTEEN

BIBLE PASSAGE

Daniel 6:13, 16-21

Then they said to the king, "Daniel, one of the exiles from Judah, does not respect Your Majesty or obey the order you issued. He prays regularly three times a day."

So the king gave orders for Daniel to be taken and thrown into the pit filled with lions. He said to Daniel, "May your God, whom you serve so loyally, rescue you." A stone was put over the mouth of the pit, and the king placed his own royal seal and the seal of his noblemen on the stone, so that no one could rescue Daniel. Then the king returned to the palace and spent a sleepless night, without food or any form of entertainment.

At dawn the king got up and hurried to the pit. When he got there, he called out anxiously, "Daniel, servant of the living God! Was the God you serve so loyally able to save you from the lions?"

Daniel answered, "May Your Majesty live forever! God sent his angel to shut the mouths of the lions so that they would not hurt me. He did this because he knew that I was innocent and because I have not wronged you, Your Majesty."

DEVOTIONAL

Daniel and the Lions

Did you know that in some places in the world today, you can get into lots of trouble just for being a Christian? If you carry a Bible, or go to church, or talk about Jesus, you could end up in prison – and sometimes get hurt badly, as well.

Today we learn about Daniel, who is in a similar position. It's against the law to pray to God in the country he lives in – but he still does it. And he gets into a whole load of trouble, doesn't he? A den of lions doesn't sound all that much fun...

But something incredible happens. The lions leave him alone, instead of gobbling him up for their dinner, because an angel comes to keep Daniel safe. The next morning, he's found completely untouched, sitting there in the middle of all those lions.

Years later, God sent Jesus to rescue all of us, just as he sent the angel for Daniel. Jesus came so that we are able to be in relationship with God at any time, whether or not the rules in our country allow it. And that's why persecuted Christians still pray; because they know God is with them and for them. Hallelujah!

PRAY

Jesus, we pray for those Christians who are in prison and persecuted for their faith. Fill them with peace and courage. And keep us strong in you, as well, fill us with boldness to tell others about you and to pray, even when it is hard. Amen.

THINK

Have you ever been picked on or discriminated against for your faith? How did you feel? How do you think your witness at that time impacted you, and those around you?

DO

It was Daniel's custom to kneel down under his open windows, and pray. Why don't you have a go? Open one of the windows in your house, and kneel on the floor next to it, and then pray – for all you can see, for all that lies beyond your view, and for everything that is worrying you right now.

She will
BRING
Peace

———

DAY
NINETEEN

DEVOTIONAL

Prophecy of a Saviour to be born in Bethlehem

BIBLE PASSAGE

Micah 5:1-5
People of Jerusalem, gather your forces! We are besieged! They are attacking the leader of Israel!
The Lord says, "Bethlehem Ephrathah, you are one of the smallest towns in Judah, but out of you I will bring a ruler for Israel, whose family line goes back to ancient times."
So the Lord will abandon his people to their enemies until the woman who is to give birth has her son. Then those Israelites who are in exile will be reunited with their own people. When he comes, he will rule his people with the strength that comes from the Lord and with the majesty of the Lord God himself. His people will live in safety because people all over the earth will acknowledge his greatness, and he will bring peace.

In this amazing passage, we find a guy who lived 700 years before Jesus talking about Jesus' birth – isn't that incredible? Even though it was just people like you and me who wrote the words of the Bible, it was God who inspired those words – and God inspired a whole load of prophecies like Micah's one here, about Jesus, the coming Messiah.

Micah gives a wonderful picture of who this Messiah will be. He will reconcile people, rule with strength and majesty, and bring peace and safety to his people. And we know that when Jesus came to earth, he did all of those things – and still does today. Through his Holy Spirit, poured out on all, we can all live in Jesus' majesty, greatness and peace.

DIVE DEEPER
1 Samuel 7:12
Romans 15:4

PRAY

Lord, thank you that you inspired people to write down your words of truth in the Bible, and thank you that we can read these words today. Thank you that you gave prophets amazing pictures of events hundreds of years before they would happen. We pray that you would pour out your Holy Spirit on us today, that others will see the majesty and greatness of Jesus shining through us. Amen.

THINK

Why do you think Jesus was born in a small, unknown town, Bethlehem, and then grew up in a small, unknown village, Nazareth? Can you think of any other examples in the Bible or in your life where God has used small things for a greater purpose?

DO

Search through the passage, and find the words that describe Jesus. You could even go to other parts of the Bible! Write them down above each other to make a graffiti wall 'Ebenezer', a towering reminder of who God is. If you're feeling creative, use stones, bricks, or even a jenga tower instead. It might even look a bit like a mini Bethlehem...

I stand in the presence of God, who sent me to speak to you and tell you this good news

DAY
TWENTY

BIBLE PASSAGE

Luke 1:8-15

One day Zechariah was doing his work as a priest in the Temple, taking his turn in the daily service. According to the custom followed by the priests, he was chosen by lot to burn incense on the altar. So he went into the Temple of the Lord, while the crowd of people outside prayed during the hour when the incense was burned.

An angel of the Lord appeared to him, standing at the right side of the altar where the incense was burned. When Zechariah saw him, he was alarmed and felt afraid. But the angel said to him, "Don't be afraid, Zechariah! God has heard your prayer, and your wife Elizabeth will bear you a son. You are to name him John. How glad and happy you will be, and how happy many others will be when he is born! John will be great in the Lord's sight."

DEVOTIONAL

Elizabeth and Zechariah

I wonder how often you have been to church? For lots of us, it's something we often do on a Sunday – if not in person, online!

Imagine you're in church, and halfway through singing the first song. All is normal. You're singing away, enjoying the worship, when all of a sudden – BOOM! – An angel appears right in front of the communion table! WOW! How do you think you'd feel? What would you be thinking?

Today we see exactly this happening to Zechariah. He's on his own, just going about his usual business in the temple where he works, when suddenly, out of nowhere, an angel shows up! The angel assures him that God has heard his prayer, and that he will have the child he and his wife Elizabeth so long for. That child will grow up to be John the Baptist, who will tell everyone about Jesus, preparing the way for him. What an incredible answer to prayer!

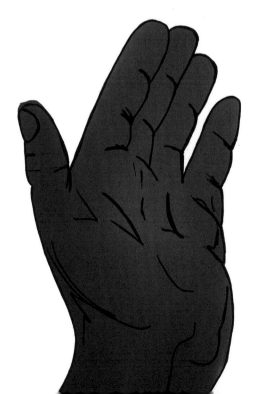
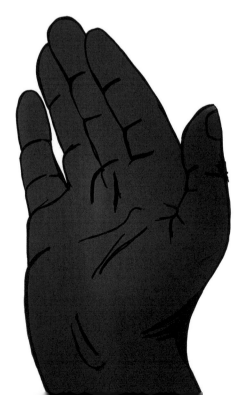

PRAY

God, please help us to persevere in prayer even when it's hard, knowing that you hear us and answer. We pray that your Holy Spirit will break through into our lives and communities, bringing new life. Amen.

THINK

Have you ever experienced a very tangible glimpse of heaven? Maybe you saw or sensed an angel, or perhaps you encountered God's presence so heavily upon you and around you that everything else seemed to stop, even time, and it was just you and God in that moment. Hold that experience before you: what changed in you? Why do you think God chose that moment to show up so spectacularly?

DO

Get your hands on some party poppers, or get hold of some balloons or paper bags. Littlies, make sure your grown up is helping you! Play your favourite worship song, and then set off the poppers, burst your balloons, or smash your paper bags – and think about the way the angel so suddenly appeared to Zechariah!

DAY
TWENTYONE

BIBLE PASSAGE

DEVOTIONAL

Matthew 3:1-6

John the Baptist

At that time John the Baptist came to the desert of Judea and started preaching. "Turn away from your sins," he said, "because the Kingdom of heaven is near!" John was the man the prophet Isaiah was talking about when he said, "Someone is shouting in the desert, 'Prepare a road for the Lord; make a straight path for him to travel!'" John's clothes were made of camel's hair; he wore a leather belt around his waist, and his food was locusts and wild honey. People came to him from Jerusalem, from the whole province of Judea, and from all over the country near the Jordan River. They confessed their sins, and he baptized them in the Jordan.

Not long ago, I went out to Ellesmere Lake to baptize a couple of people. It was freezing cold! Unlike John, I wasn't wearing clothes made of camel's hair, or even a leather belt – and, afterwards, we went to the café for tea and cake, not locusts and honey, thankfully! We had a great time celebrating with two friends who were publicly declaring their faith. We drew quite a crowd as they confessed their sin, turned to Jesus, and plunged under the water.

This symbolism – plunging down under the water, then rising up out of it – reminds us that we leave our old lives behind, and rise again to new life in Jesus. The old has gone and the new has come.

DIVE DEEPER
Isaiah 40:3-6
Acts 13:24-25

PRAY

Lord, thank you for the gift of baptism, and the new life that you offer us. Thank you that you help us to die to sin and live for you, and for how you died for all our sin, and rose in glory. Amen.

DO

This will be messy! Get your hands in some muddy wet soil, and work the mud into the cracks in your skin. Leave it there for as long as you can bear it. Finally, plunge your hands into warm soapy water, and scrub them clean, thinking about how Jesus does this to our hearts.

THINK

If you have been baptized, think back to that day if you can. Remember the emotions. How did you feel before you went under the water? And what about when you came up? And if you haven't been baptised – spend a moment thinking about it. Do you think you'd like to be?

THANK YOU JESUS FOR WASHING ME CLEAN.

_____

DAY
TWENTYTWO

BIBLE PASSAGE

Luke 1:26-31

In the sixth month of Elizabeth's pregnancy God sent the angel Gabriel to a town in Galilee named Nazareth. He had a message for a young woman promised in marriage to a man named Joseph, who was a descendant of King David. Her name was Mary. The angel came to her and said, "Peace be with you! The Lord is with you and has greatly blessed you!"
Mary was deeply troubled by the angel's message, and she wondered what his words meant. The angel said to her, "Don't be afraid, Mary; God has been gracious to you. You will become pregnant and give birth to a son, and you will name him Jesus. He will be great and will be called the Son of the Most High God. The Lord God will make him a king, as his ancestor David was, and he will be the king of the descendants of Jacob forever; his kingdom will never end!"

DIVE DEEPER
Hebrews 13:2
Genesis 18:2

DEVOTIONAL

God chooses Mary

Literally half an hour ago, we had a knock on the door from some lovely friends with a box of chocolates for us. We were surprised to see them, excited by the present, and felt pleased that they had thought of us!

Remember the angel's surprise visit to Zechariah the other day? Today we have another visit – this time, to Mary, who is afraid, and can't understand why the angel has come to see her, of all people, just a young girl.

The angel has some incredible – and scary – news for Mary. She – just a teenager – will become pregnant, and give birth to a baby son, who will be named Jesus, the King of an everlasting kingdom! Mary is astounded at the news. How could she have a baby? But she chooses to trust God, and tells the angel that she will do as God asks. Then the angel leaves – just like that. How must Mary have felt?

PRAY

Thank you Lord for nice surprises that help us feel loved and special. And thank you that you visited Mary – and that she trusted you. Help us to trust you with our lives, like she trusted you with hers. Amen.

THINK

Have you ever had a surprise visit? Who was it? Did they bring anything? How did you feel afterwards?

DO

Random act of kindness time!
You could bake a cake for a mystery neighbour, leave flowers on a doorstop somewhere, or pay for the person behind you at the drive through. As you do this, pray that they might be surprised by the love of God, and his Spirit making himself known to them.

"FOR THERE IS NOTHING THAT GOD CANNOT DO"

HE WILL BE CALLED IMMANUEL

DAY
TWENTY-THREE

DEVOTIONAL

BIBLE PASSAGE

Matthew 1:18-21
This was how the birth of Jesus Christ took place. His mother Mary was engaged to Joseph, but before they were married, she found out that she was going to have a baby by the Holy Spirit. Joseph was a man who always did what was right, but he did not want to disgrace Mary publicly; so he made plans to break the engagement privately. While he was thinking about this, an angel of the Lord appeared to him in a dream and said, "Joseph, descendant of David, do not be afraid to take Mary to be your wife. For it is by the Holy Spirit that she has conceived. She will have a son, and you will name him Jesus because he will save his people from their sins."

Angel appears to Joseph
It's yet another surprise angelic visit today – this time, to Joseph, to tell him the unexpected news that his fiancé, Mary, is pregnant! How do you think he would have felt, hearing this news?

Today, many couples have children before getting married, but in those days it wasn't usual, and people would have been very unkind to Mary and Joseph, picking on them and spreading gossip about them. They might have been ignored or even bullied by their own friends and family. Yet they kept trusting God through all of this, staying true to him.

If you've even been bullied, or picked on, or gossiped about, you know that it can make you feel very sad. Remember that just as God was with Mary and Joseph, he is with you, too, and loves you.

DIVE DEEPER
Judges 13:6-21
Isaiah 26:3-4

PRAY

Lord, when we go through difficult times, or when others are unkind to us, picking on us and making us feel unhappy, help us to trust that you are by our side and that you love us more than we can imagine. Holy Spirit, fall upon us and remind us that you are here. Amen.

THINK

Hold in your mind a time when you felt picked on, or even bullied. What was it that caused that feeling? What would you say to someone who was going through the same thing today that might help them? How does your faith help you in times like this?

DO

Children will need to ask an adult to help with this one. Find a piece of paper and write down a few words about a time you felt bullied, or unkind words others have said about you. Now, give these words over to God by burning the paper in a firepit or by lighting it with a match in the garden. Watch how it burns up, and remember that God can take away these words forever.

GOD IS ALWAYS WITH US, AND HE LOVES US.

he was a
DESCENDANT
of David

DAY
TWENTYFOUR

BIBLE PASSAGE

Luke 2:1-5
At that time Emperor Augustus ordered a census to be taken throughout the Roman Empire. When this first census took place, Quirinius was the governor of Syria. Everyone, then, went to register himself, each to his own hometown. Joseph went from the town of Nazareth in Galilee to the town of Bethlehem in Judea, the birthplace of King David. Joseph went there because he was a descendant of David. He went to register with Mary, who was promised in marriage to him. She was pregnant.

DEVOTIONAL

Mary and Joseph go to Bethlehem
Do you remember at the beginning of Advent, we talked about a long journey that Abram went on – leaving everything he knew to go to a new place?

Today we go on another long journey with some different people. Mary and Joseph walked for around 90 miles – more than from Telford to Birmingham and back again. How do you think your feet would feel after a long hike like that? Ouch!

They walked and they walked, through day and night, and, finally, weary and anxious, they reached Bethlehem – the town Micah had prophesied about so many years before.

Traipsing through the desolate land, they would have carried all their fears with them – and their hopes and dreams, too. They would have plenty of time to share them with one another as they walked.

Isn't it good that, on the journey of life, with all its ups and downs, hopes and fears, that God is always, always with us.

DIVE DEEPER
John 7:42
Luke 24:13-35

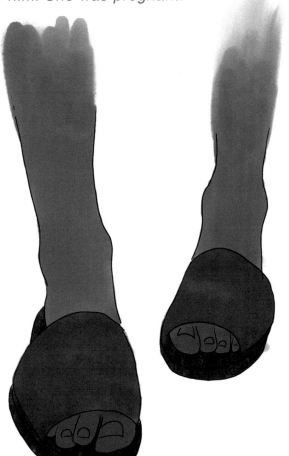

PRAY

Lord, we thank you for Mary and Joseph's trust in you. Help us, too, to trust in you, especially when the going gets tough. Amen.

THINK

How do you think Mary and Joseph would have felt starting on their journey? What might they have talked about as they walked to Bethlehem? What do you think worried them?

DO

Decide on a prayer word you want to take through the day with you. Maybe it could be hope, or blessing, peace, or reconciliation. Then write it on the sole of your shoe, and remember that everywhere you go the word is going with you, leaving an imprint of your prayer.

WHERE DID YOU WALK?

"don't be afraid I am here with good news"

DAY
TWENTYFIVE

Luke 2:6-13

While they were in Bethlehem, the time came for her to have her baby. She gave birth to her first son, wrapped him in cloths and laid him in a manger—there was no room for them to stay in the inn. There were some shepherds in that part of the country who were spending the night in the fields, taking care of their flocks. An angel of the Lord appeared to them, and the glory of the Lord shone over them. They were terribly afraid, but the angel said to them, "Don't be afraid! I am here with good news for you, which will bring great joy to all the people. This very day in David's town your Saviour was born—Christ the Lord! And this is what will prove it to you: you will find a baby wrapped in cloths and lying in a manger."

Suddenly a great army of heaven's angels appeared with the angel, singing praises to God:

"Glory to God in the highest heaven,
and peace on earth to those with whom he is pleased!"

DEVOTIONAL

Jesus is born

Think about when you're in the cinema, watching an incredible film, or an awesome play at the theatre. Think about that feeling you get when it comes to the big finale, where everything gets wrapped up, all the music and visuals swelling to a spectacular ending that leaves you breathless.

This story might feel a bit like this. We've got the angels appearing again, praising God. We've got a bunch or shepherds too, also praising God. And then we've got this brand new baby, named Jesus – a name that reminds us that God is with us.

Is that it, though? Is that the glorious finale, the final curtain, the end of the story? Well, no... not at all. This is when things begin to build up to that excitement we feel towards the end of a great story – but it's only the beginning of the end. This is when we start bursting with hope, when we know God has come down among us, when the potential for a life with Jesus is laid out before us.

Today, that offer is open to all – to walk with Jesus, to embrace the new life he brings, to join the angels and shepherds in worship around the manger. Jesus Christ, once a baby in Bethlehem, now the King of glory.

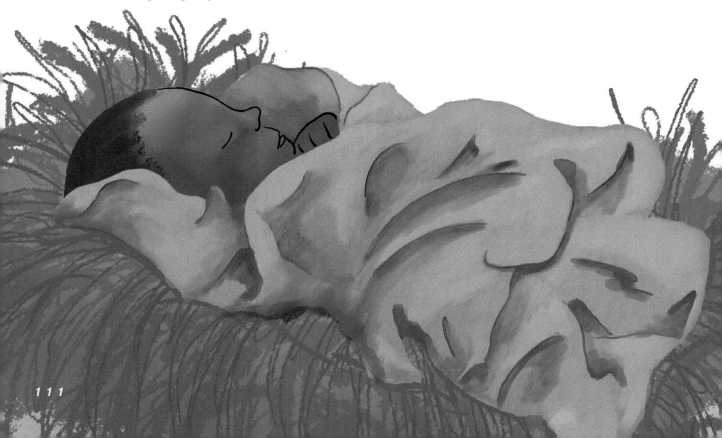

PRAY

Lord Jesus, we do worship at your manger, laying our lives before you. We join with the angels, shepherds, and millions through history as we declare you the wonderful counsellor, prince of peace, and almighty God. This Christmas, may we know you more, love you more, and live for you more. In Jesus' name, Amen.

THINK

As an unmarried teenage mum, how do you think Mary would have felt going back to Joseph's home town – potentially staying with his family in their home? What conversation do you think the shepherds had with Mary? How do you think the lives of the shepherds were changed?

DO

You might be lucky enough to have some gifts today. They won't stay wrapped up forever – in fact, the whole point is that they are opened and enjoyed. In a similar way, Jesus offers us a new life that needs to be unwrapped, and open – so as you open gifts, and throw the wrapping paper away, say thank you to God for his goodness, and for the way he transforms your life, getting rid of all the rubbish.

DIVE DEEPER
Revelation 12:1-5
John 1:14

WHAT'S BEEN THE HIGHLIGHT OF THIS MONTH FOR YOU?
WHAT'S CHALLENGED YOU?
HOW HAS YOUR WALK WITH JESUS CHANGED?

ACKNOWLEDGEMENTS

In the words of Ecclesiastes 1:9, there is nothing new under the sun. This book is full of ideas and thoughts which have, no doubt, been influenced by numerous people which I have had the pleasure of doing life with.

The Bible readings themselves were selected by Rev'd. Tim Carter, vicar at All Saints, Wellington with St. Catherine's, Eyton, for the advent season in 2020.

Caroline Gwilliam, a friend and colleague, helped me with some of the activities for the 'Do' section, and her creativity was much appreciated!

On day 24, the activity involving writing on the sole of your shoe was adapted from Sole Prayers, by Gerard Kelly on the Bless Network. You can find out more at blessnet.eu.

Many thanks, and chocolatey gifts, are due to (in no particular order) Thomas Creedy, Abby Guinness, Liz Carter, Lucy Rycroft, and Bob Hartman, for their help and time throughout the publishing process.

ABOUT THE ILLUSTRATORS & DESIGNERS

The Illustrators and Designers of this beautiful study book are Hope Gwilliam and Becky Rawlins who are friends of David's. They are graduates in surface pattern design from Staffordshire University and co-own and run Hopefully Made, an earth friendly company, specialising in hand screen printing. They are both talented artists who are passionate about illustration. They have previously illustrated Supercharged Superhero, a children's book written by Gemma Everson. This is the first study book that they have worked on, and have enjoyed bringing life to these famous moments in history.

HOPEFULLY_MADE
WEAREHOPEFULLYMADE.COM

ABOUT THE AUTHOR

The Author of this book is David Sims, who lives in the Midlands with his wonderful, crazy family. He is married to the ever patient Kimberley and has three young children, A, E and S. David is a leader in the Church of England. Previously to this he spent 9 years teaching geography to teenagers. Little did he know he was being prepared for a life of teaching the gospel, and sharing God's love! While he is not working, he spends time in his local coffee shops enjoying great coffee and calorific breakfasts.

He is passionate about getting the church excited for Jesus, and showing all of God's people, big and small, that they have a ministry, a calling, and that the things of the holy spirit are for every, single follower of Jesus. This passion and love has called him to encourage the church to rise up and love vulnerable children. He has previously worked with Home for Good, a Christian adoption organistion, who are working to find homes for all vulnerable children. All of God's children deserve to be loved as He loves us.

CREATIONTOCRIB